CHRISTMAS FAVORITES

Solos and Band Arrangements
Correlated with Essential Elements Band Method

ARRANGED BY
MICHAEL SWEENEY

Welcome to Essential Elements Christmas Favorites! There are two versions of each holiday selection in this versatile book:
1. The SOLO version (with lyrics) appears on the left-hand page.
2. The FULL BAND arrangement appears on the right-hand page.

Use the optional accompaniment tape when playing solos for friends and family. Your director may also use the accompaniment tape in band rehearsals and concerts.

ISBN 0-7935-1753-2

HAL•LEONARD®
CORPORATION
7777 W. BLUEMOUND RD. P.O. BOX 13819 MILWAUKEE, WI 53213

00862502

JINGLE BELLS

Words and Music by J. PIERPONT
Arranged by MICHAEL SWEENEY

Solo

Introduction

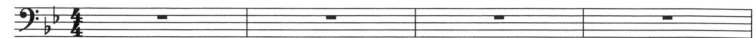

Jin - gle Bells, Jin - gle Bells, Jin - gle all the way.

Oh what fun it is to ride in a one horse o - pen sleigh!

Jin - gle Bells, Jin - gle Bells, Jin - gle all the way.

Oh what fun it is to ride in a one horse o - pen sleigh!

Interlude

Oh what fun it is to ride in a one horse o - pen sleigh!

00862502

JINGLE BELLS

Words and Music by J. PIERPONT
Arranged by MICHAEL SWEENEY

Band Arrangement

00862502

UP ON THE HOUSETOP

Arranged by MICHAEL SWEENEY

Solo

UP ON THE HOUSETOP

Band Arrangement

Arranged by MICHAEL SWEENEY

00862502

THE HANUKKAH SONG

Arranged by MICHAEL SWEENEY

Solo

THE HANUKKAH SONG

Band Arrangement

Arranged by MICHAEL SWEENEY

00862502

A HOLLY JOLLY CHRISTMAS

Music and Lyrics by JOHNNY MARKS
Arranged by MICHAEL SWEENEY

Solo

A HOLLY JOLLY CHRISTMAS

Music and Lyrics by JOHNNY MARKS
Arranged by MICHAEL SWEENEY

Band Arrangement

WE WISH YOU A MERRY CHRISTMAS

Solo

Arranged by MICHAEL SWEENEY

WE WISH YOU A MERRY CHRISTMAS

Band Arrangement

Arranged by MICHAEL SWEENEY

00862502

FROSTY THE SNOW MAN

Words and Music by STEVE NELSON and JACK ROLLINS
Arranged by MICHAEL SWEENEY

Solo

FROSTY THE SNOW MAN

Words and Music by STEVE NELSON and JACK ROLLINS
Arranged by MICHAEL SWEENEY

Band Arrangement

00862502

ROCKIN' AROUND THE CHRISTMAS TREE

Music and Lyrics by JOHNNY MARKS
Arranged by MICHAEL SWEENEY

Solo

ROCKIN' AROUND THE CHRISTMAS TREE

Music and Lyrics by JOHNNY MARKS
Arranged by MICHAEL SWEENEY

Band Arrangement

00862502

JINGLE-BELL ROCK

Words and Music by JOE BEAL and JIM BOOTHE
Arranged by MICHAEL SWEENEY

Solo

JINGLE-BELL ROCK

**Words and Music by JOE BEAL
and JIM BOOTHE**

Arranged by MICHAEL SWEENEY

Band Arrangement

RUDOLPH THE RED-NOSED REINDEER

Music and Lyrics by JOHNNY MARKS
Arranged by MICHAEL SWEENEY

Solo

Introduction - Moderately Slow

You know Dash-er and Danc-er and Pranc-er and Vix-en, Com-et and Cu-pid and Don-ner and Blitz-en, but do you re-call the most fa-mous rein-deer of all.

11 Moderate Bossa

Ru-dolph, the red-nosed rein-deer had a ver-y shin-y nose, and if you ev-er saw it, you would e-ven say it glows.

19 f All of the oth-er rein-deer used to laugh and call him names, they nev-er let poor Ru-dolph join in an-y rein-deer games.

27 mf Then one fog-gy Christ-mas Eve, San-ta came to say, "Ru-dolph, with your nose so bright, won't you guide my sleigh to-night?" Then how the rein-deer loved him

35 f as they shout-ed out with glee: "Ru-dolph, the red-nosed rein-deer, you'll go down in his-to-

1. ry!"

2. you'll go down in his-to-ry!"

RUDOLPH THE RED-NOSED REINDEER

Music and Lyrics by JOHNNY MARKS
Arranged by MICHAEL SWEENEY

Band Arrangement

LET IT SNOW!
Let It Snow! Let It Snow!

Words by SAMMY CAHN
Music by JULE STYNE
Arranged by MICHAEL SWEENEY

Solo

Lyrics under the music:

Oh the weath-er out-side is fright-ful But the fire is so de-light-ful, And since we've no place to go, Let it snow! Let it snow! Let it snow! It does-n't show signs of stop-ping, And I brought some corn for pop-ping, The lights are turned way down low, Let it snow! Let it snow! Let it snow! When we fi-nal-ly kiss good-night, How I'll hate go-ing out in the storm! But if you'll real-ly hold me tight, All the way home I'll be warm. The fire is slow-ly dy-ing And my dear we're still good-bye-ing, But as long as you love me so, Let it snow! Let it snow! Let it snow! When we snow!

LET IT SNOW! LET IT SNOW! LET IT SNOW!

Band Arrangement

Words by SAMMY CAHN
Music by JULE STYNE
Arranged by MICHAEL SWEENEY

THE CHRISTMAS SONG

Music and Lyric by MEL TORME and ROBERT WELLS

Arranged by MICHAEL SWEENEY

Solo

THE CHRISTMAS SONG

Music and Lyric by MEL TORME and ROBERT WELLS

Arranged by MICHAEL SWEENEY

Band Arrangement

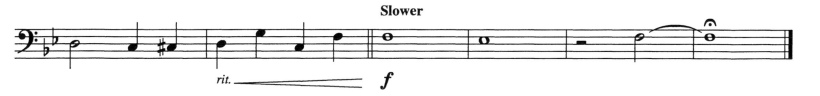

00862502